For Paul Nagrowski and his Grandpa Irving—T. S.
To Trish and our parents—R. C.
Special thanks to David Abrahamson, text consultant.

THE BIG BOOK OF REAL
RACE CARS
AND RACE CAR DRIVING

By Teddy Slater

Illustrated by Richard Courtney

Grosset & Dunlap • New York

Copyright © 1989 by Grosset & Dunlap, Inc. All rights reserved. Published by Grosset & Dunlap, Inc., a member of The Putnam Publishing Group, New York. Published simultaneously in Canada. Printed in Hong Kong. Library of Congress Catalog Card Number: 87-82638 ISBN 0-448-19187-3 Reinforced Binding A B C D E F G H I J

FAST, FASTER, FASTEST
Record Breaking Cars of the Past

Speed (mph)	Year	Driver/Car	Country
39.24	1898	Chasseloup-Laubat/Jeantaud	France
65.79	1899	Jenatzy/La Jamais Contente	France
75.06	1902	Serpollet/Serpollet	France
91.37	1904	Ford/Ford Arrow	USA
103.55	1904	Rigolly/Gobron-Brillié	Belgium
127.66	1906	Marriot/Stanley Rocket	USA
150.87	1925	Campbell/Sunbeam	Wales
203.79	1927	Segrave/Sunbeam	USA
253.97	1932	Campbell/Bluebird Napier	USA
301.13	1935	Campbell/Bluebird Rolls-Royce	USA
350.20	1938	Cobb/Railton	USA
407.45	1963	Breedlove/Spirit of America*	USA
526.28	1964	Breedlove/Spirit of America*	USA
576.553	1965	Arfons/Green Monster*	USA
600.601	1965	Breedlove/Spirit of America —Sonic I*	USA
622.407	1970	Gabelich/Blue Flame*	USA
633.468	1983	Noble/Thrust 2*	USA
739.666	1983	Barrett/Budweiser Rocket*	USA

* Jet- or rocket-engine cars

Imagine a cheering, screaming crowd of 200,000 fans, powerful car engines shrieking into high gear, and a green flag wildly waving to urge drivers on. This is the start of one of the toughest and most demanding sports around—automobile racing. It is a sport that tests the limits of a driver's skill and endurance (and the performance of his or her race car), against the sometimes narrow tracks, poor road conditions, and high speeds that threaten to cause serious collisions.

All over the world automobile racing is a popular sport. Cars range in shape and size, and races last from just a few seconds over a short distance to several weeks going from country to country. Many drivers compete in different races all year long.

Not all race cars compete in standard racing events. The *Budweiser Rocket* was designed to satisfy the desire for pure speed only. The car is a strange-looking three-wheeled vehicle, 39 feet long and less than 2 feet wide. In December 1979, the *Budweiser Rocket* raced against the time clock and broke the sound barrier by reaching the incredible speed of 739 mph for a land-speed record. That's as fast as some jets fly. No wonder—the *Budweiser Rocket* has a 50,000-horsepower jet engine!

Racing in the Past

When automobile racing began, in the 1890s, the new "horseless carriages" were no faster than the best horse and buggies of the day. Emil Levassor won the first major road race in 1895. It was a 732-mile round trip from Paris to Bordeaux, France. Levassor's car averaged only 15mph.

The bullet-shaped *La Jamais Contente* (French for "the never satisfied") was the first car to reach the 60 mph mark. In 1889 it reached the speed of 62 mph, a land-speed record it held for three years.

The earliest races were held on ordinary roads, which were often rough and bumpy and unpaved. Clouds of blinding dust, and even an occasional animal attack, made racing a most difficult and dangerous sport. In the 1903 Paris-Madrid race, later known as the "Race of Death," so many drivers, mechanics, and spectators were killed that the race had to be stopped. Race car driver Marcel Renault was speeding along in his car at 80 mph when he crashed.

The *Locomobile Old 16* was the first American car fast enough to compete with the European racers. In 1908 it outraced them all to win the Vanderbilt Cup, America's first international racing victory.

After the Paris-Madrid disaster, most races were held on closed circuits or oval tracks. At the first Indianapolis 500 in 1911, winner Ray Harroun drove a *Marmon Wasp* 200 times around a 2½-mile oval. He averaged 74.59 mph. The Marmon was not only the fastest car in the race, but it was also the only car to have a rearview mirror. It was a brand-new safety feature that would soon be required equipment for all automobiles.

In the 1920s the *Bugatti Type 35* was the fastest of the Grand Prix or international racing cars. Between 1925 and 1927, Bugattis won almost 2,000 races.

This 1927 *Sunbeam* broke the 120 mph mark. Powered by two giant airplane engines, it was built especially for a land-speed record and reached a maximum speed of 124 mph.

By 1970 the fastest car on the race track was the *Porsche 917*. It had a top speed of 235 mph and averaged 162 mph in competition.

Formula Racing

Formula One cars are the most expensive of all the Formula Cars. A formula is a set of rules and regulations that limits the size and weight of the various kinds of cars and their engines. Overall chassis or body design, type of fuel used, safety equipment, and even the length of the race are all part of the formula. Everything down to the last detail must meet the strictest standards.

Every Formula One car is truly one of a kind. Each of these racers is individually designed and manufactured. These rear-engine cars have only one seat, an open cockpit, and open wheels—that is, no fenders.

The design of Formula Ones features front and rear airfoils which work like upside-down aircraft wings. Aircraft wings create a force that lifts a plane for flying. Race car wings create a force that presses a car down to the road. This helps the wheels grip the track better and allows the car to take turns at very high speeds. These sleek-looking cars sit very low to the ground. The seat in a Formula Car racer is a tight space just behind the front wheels. It allows the driver to lie back and feel like part of the car when it moves.

The **Monaco Grand Prix** is the most glamorous of all auto races. The Grand Prix (pronounced *grahn* PREE) is a series of international road races for Formula One cars, which are also known as Grand Prix cars. (The French term *Grand Prix* means "large prize.") The winner of the series is crowned the World Driving Champion. Grand Prix races are held on extremely challenging courses, where the cars may go as fast as 200 mph on the straightaways, or straight parts of the road, and as slowly as 30 mph on the sharpest curves.

At the Monaco Grand Prix the cars race along the public roadways of Monte Carlo. On race day, of course, the roads are closed to regular traffic. With the exception of this race and the U.S. Grand Prix in Detroit, Michigan, most of the other races in this series are held on specially built tracks or courses.

Other Formula cars include the **Formula Two**, which looks very much like the Formula One but is only three-quarters the size. The engine is smaller, too, and it doesn't go as fast.

One step down from the Formula Two is the **Formula Three** car. It not only has a smaller engine than the Formula One, but its tires are narrower and its wings are smaller. Most of today's best Grand Prix drivers began their careers in Formula Three racing.

Drag Racing

Drag races or meets are held on straight, paved tracks called drag strips. Although hundreds of cars may compete in a single drag meet, they race only two at a time, side by side. The loser of each round, or heat, is eliminated from the competition. The winner advances to race against another car until only two cars are left. The winner of the last round is the champion.

Top Fuel Cars are the most popular of all drag racers, with their rear engines, single seats, and long slender frames. These dragsters, as they're also called, have small front wheels and large rear ones because most of the car's weight shifts to the back during acceleration. From a standing start, the fastest car can reach speeds of more than 260 mph on the short quarter-mile track. Top Fuel cars go so fast that from start to finish the race is less than 6 seconds long. What's more, they need parachutes to help them stop!

Funny Cars are another kind of drag racer. They look like a stretched-out version of a regular passenger car. Funny cars can go as fast as 260 mph. They are fueled by a special mixture of a poisonous liquid called nitromethane and alcohol. These front-engine racers are covered by a very lightweight, one-piece plastic body. That means there are no doors. The driver enters and leaves the car by simply flipping up the whole body.

Stock Car Racing

Stock Cars resemble ordinary passenger cars on the outside, but they are quite different on the inside. The builder of one of these cars starts with a large, late-model sedan like those a neighborhood car dealer has in stock. Then the engine is taken apart and completely rebuilt. To safely withstand the higher speeds of the now improved or "souped-up" engine, the rest of the car is also strengthened. A heavy-duty frame or "cage" of thick steel tubing is welded inside the car's body. Then the car's suspension system (for road bumps), as well as its steering and brakes, are secured to this frame.

Although stock cars weigh more than twice as much as Formula One cars, the large, powerful stock car engines allow them to go more than 200 mph on the straightaways. Unlike Formula cars, stock cars have a front engine, fenders, and a windshield. The driver sits almost upright, in the normal driving position, instead of nearly lying down.

The **Daytona 500**, held annually in Daytona Beach, Florida, is one of stock car racing's most exciting events. Here, some of the fastest stock cars roar 200 times around a 2½-mile oval track. The Daytona Speedway's wide, high-banked corners allow many cars to take the curves at speeds over 200 mph!

Nothing thrills Speedway spectators more than a maneuver known as *drafting*. This occurs when a driver gets behind another car and rides extremely close to its tail around and around the track. The front or lead car does more work by breaking the wind resistance. But the driver in the draft of air behind the lead car receives what amounts to a free ride or tow. The drafter maintains the exact same speed as the leader while saving a lot of fuel—and a lot of wear and tear on the engine.

When the drafter wants to pass the lead car, he quickly breaks away from the airstream by moving left or right. Then he presses the gas pedal to the floor for maximum speed and surges past his rival. This tactic, called *slingshotting*, is used most dramatically on the very last lap of a race.

Pit Stop

In a long race like the Daytona 500, the cars take a terrible beating. Tires must be changed three or more times, especially those on the right side of the car. These "outside" tires get the most wear and tear in the four left turns of Daytona's race track. Fuel must be replaced every 100 miles or so, windshields cleaned, and major and minor repairs made as necessary. All this takes place in the "pits," an area alongside the track. There, specially trained crews do their best to get the cars back in action as quickly as possible. Each car and driver has its own pit crew. In a race where every second counts, a good pit crew can mean the difference between victory and defeat. A smooth stop with refueling, tire changing, and no time-consuming repairs takes only 15 seconds!

Safety First

There is no denying that automobile racing is a dangerous sport. The faster race cars travel, the more thrilling a race is for fans. But most races place limitations on a car's weight, engine power, and chassis design to lower the risk of injury to drivers. And thanks to modern technology, racing is becoming safer each year.

Drivers wear clothing that protects them from head to toe. Jumpsuits, coveralls, gloves—even underwear—are all made of a special flame-resistant material.

The most important safety gear a driver owns is his helmet. It has a hard fiberglass outer shell and a soft, foam-cushioned lining. A good helmet might cost $500, but a driver rarely complains about this expense. When it comes to safety, a helmet is priceless.

All race car drivers wear safety harnesses. They are standard equipment on racing cars. The special "six-point" belts feature two straps across the driver's shoulders and one strap across the lap—all connected with a single quick-release buckle.

Race cars have built-in devices to protect the driver's upper body in a crash. Roofless cars, such as the Formula racers, come equipped with roll bars positioned behind the seat. These metal bars (shaped like an upside-down "U") protect a driver if the car flips over.

Cars with roofs, such as stock cars and Funny Cars, feature a roll cage—a steel-tube structure that prevents the roof of an overturned car from collapsing.

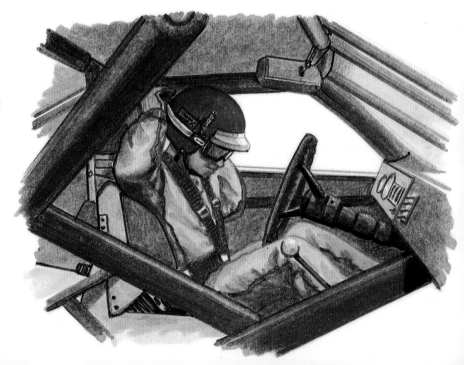

The drivers aren't the only ones who must be protected. Track officials are just as concerned with the fans' safety. Strong guardrails, reinforced concrete walls, and heavy fencing make it possible for racing fans to enjoy the thrills and spills of this most exciting sport—from a safe distance.

If all else fails, safety crews are always on call. Ambulances and even helicopters may be available to rush the injured to a hospital.

Tow trucks clear disabled cars and unwanted materials from the track before they become a hazard to the other drivers.

With all the flammable fuel around, fire is an ever-present danger, both in the pits and on the track. At the first flicker of a flame, a well-trained team of firefighters rushes to put it out.

Dirt Track Racing

Karts are the smallest of all racing vehicles. Karts—or go-karts as they're often called—are about 5 feet long and have an open body of steel tubing, balloon tires, and chrome-steel bumpers. They are quite low to the ground, with the bench or seat just inches above the track.

Many drivers begin their careers with karts. Children as young as 8 years old compete in short races on asphalt or dirt tracks. Teenagers 16 years old may enter the longer road races. But karting isn't just for kids. Many adults compete in these speedy little race cars. Some can go over 100 mph. No matter what their age, all drivers must wear protective headgear and padded jackets to shield their upper bodies.

A **Midget Car** is a little larger—and a little faster—than a kart. Although these mini-racers may look like toys, they can zip around the track at about 115 mph. Midget races are held on dirt or asphalt quarter- or half-mile ovals, and can be as long as 25 miles (50–100 laps). Some of the most exciting events take place on indoor tracks.

A **Sprint Car** is similar to a midget but has a larger body and more powerful engine. Also, the dirt or asphalt tracks that sprint cars race on are a little longer—up to a mile around. Some sprint cars, known as *Winged Sprints*, feature a large airfoil on top of the car's roll cage. The airfoil is similar to the upside-down aircraft wings on Formula cars, but it has a plate attached to each side.

The plates help the car turn through sharp curves on the track without losing speed or overturning. One plate extends upward and forces the airflow over the car from front to rear. This helps to keep the car from turning over when it drifts sideways in the curves. The other plate extends downward to stop the airflow underneath the airfoil, which prevents the car from losing speed in the curves.

Four-Wheel-Drive Vehicles—small trucks, Jeeps, and dune buggies—compete in the rough-and-tumble world of off-road racing. These are some of the toughest machines on wheels, and they do their racing over some of the most rugged terrain on earth! The terrain includes hilly, jagged trails and dirt-track courses. Sometimes four-wheel vehicles compete in huge, specially prepared indoor arenas. But some of the most dramatic events are on the twisting and bumpy sand tracks used for motorcycle competitions.

Off-road races may last anywhere from one to 30 hours. Because they're often held in remote desert areas, these races are tests of a driver's mechanical abilities as well as his actual driving skills. There are no pit crews in the desert! The man behind the wheel has to keep his vehicle going fast—but sometimes the hardest part is just to keep it going.

Sports Car Racing

There are two basic types of sports cars: the GT racing car and the sports prototype racing car.

GT Cars start out as regular passenger cars, such as Porsches or Corvettes. Then they are completely stripped down (taken apart) and rebuilt as professional racing machines. Although doors, fenders, and windshields are left on, spare tires and other unnecessary parts are removed to make the cars lighter and faster. These racers are most often seen competing in the International Motor Sports Association (IMSA) Camel GT Championship, a series of races. Some of them are only 100 miles long, but two of the most famous races are the Daytona 24-Hour and the Sebring 12-Hour.

Sports Prototype Racing Cars are especially built for racing. Like the Formula cars, they usually feature a rear engine and large rear wing, but they have an enclosed cockpit and fenders. Sports prototype racing cars compete in the IMSA GTP ("P" for prototype) Championship. One of the most successful cars in this championship is the Porsche 962. Sports prototype racing cars also enter international endurance races. The most famous of these is held at Le Mans in France. The winner is the driver whose car completes the most laps within a specified time—in this case, 24 hours.

Collector's Items

You don't have to be a professional race car driver to own and drive a sports car. If the price is right, anyone can drive one straight out of the showroom. But these cars are expensive. The least expensive, a Toyota MR2, costs about $12,000, while a Lamborghini can cost well over $100,000!

TOYOTA MR2

CORVETTE

FERRARI

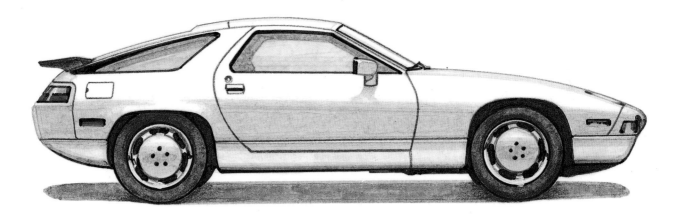

PORSCHE

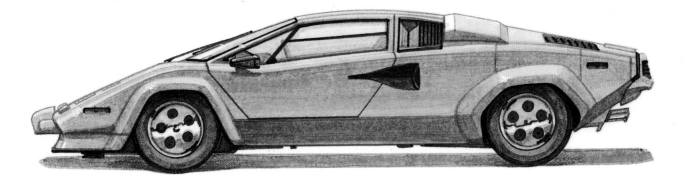

LAMBORGHINI

The 24 Hours of Le Mans

Henri is a veteran race car driver. He has won more races than he can count. But none of those victories can compare with the thrill of being one of the qualifiers in the most demanding endurance race of all—"The 24 hours of Le Mans."

It's 4:00 p.m. on a Saturday in June. Henri starts the engine of car #6, one of the nine Porsches entered in the race, and begins the first 8.4-mile lap through the French countryside. Just over 4 minutes later, he's back where he started from, flashing by the grandstands at 160 mph!

Le Mans Racing Circuit

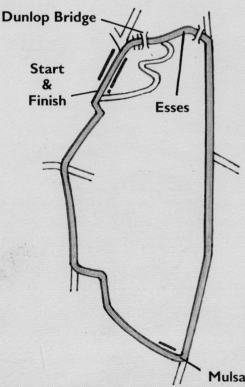

Dunlop Bridge

Start & Finish

Esses

Mulsanne Corner

Past the stands, Henri swings into a series of curves called the "Esses" at almost 100 mph. Then he follows a tree-lined road to Tours, speeding up again on the straightaway. A few miles farther, at Mulsanne Corner, he'll brake as hard as he can, taking the sharp turn at just 40 mph. Another combination of straightaways and curves brings him back to the starting line. And then another lap begins. And so it goes, hour after hour, mile after mile.

At 6:10 p.m., Henri's team manager signals him into the pit. While mechanics refuel the car, Henri's teammate, Jacques, takes his place behind the wheel. According to Le Mans rules, the same driver cannot go more than 60 laps in a row (505 miles) or drive more than 14 hours total. So racing crews are always made up of two or three drivers.

While his teammate is driving, Henri heads for a motel just behind the stands, which is reserved for the drivers. There, after a refreshing shower, he'll have something to eat—and a much-needed nap—before going back to the track to relieve Jacques.

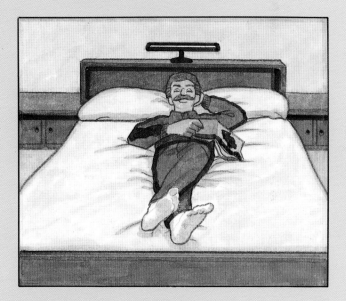

Henri and Jacques take turns driving throughout the long day and night—two hours on, two off. By 1:00 a.m. the stands and press gallery are nearly empty. Even the road is less crowded now, as one car after another drops out of the grueling race because of mechanical difficulties or accidents.

Crash! There's been a collision. An alarm sounds and a red light flashes opposite the pits. "Two cars are involved in an accident at Dunlop Bridge," the loudspeaker blares. "The cars are Jaguars #13 and #15. The drivers are unhurt, but both machines are out of the race."

Henri doesn't hear the announcement—he's wearing earplugs! But he does see and obey the yellow flag being waved by a race steward. It means, "Grave danger. No passing. Drive carefully and be ready to stop at a moment's notice." Henri and the other drivers will maintain their positions until the wreckage is cleared away and the green "go-ahead" flag waves them on.

At 3:58 p.m. the next afternoon, Henri finishes his 320th and final lap. He has driven 2,688 miles in 24 hours, averaging 112 mph. Although that puts him in 7th place, far behind the winner's 129 mph, Henri has plenty to celebrate. In a race where fewer than half the starters complete the course, just crossing the finish line is a major victory!

Indy Racing

Indy Cars are similar to Formula One racers. With their open cockpits, open wheels, and sleek, fiberglass-covered bodies, these super-speeders look almost exactly alike. But Indy cars are faster, heavier, and sturdier. They have to be. Many Indy races are 500 miles long, while Formula One races are never more than 200 miles long. Indy cars are seen at the race for which they are named—The Indianapolis 500. These cars are also known as Championship or Champ cars. They can reach speeds over 200 mph on the oval track.

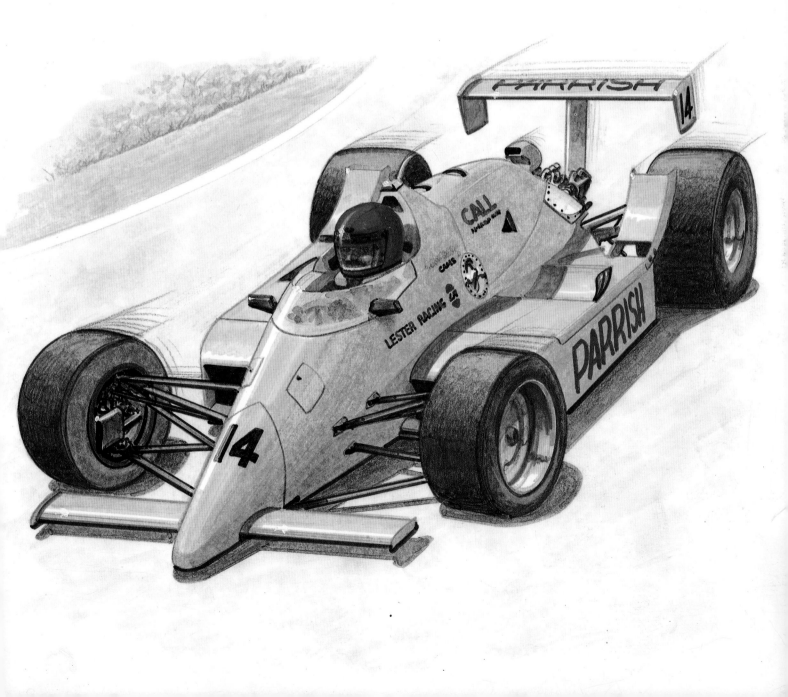

A typical Indy car is made up of about 20,000 different bits and pieces. Here's an inside look showing 30 of the most important parts.

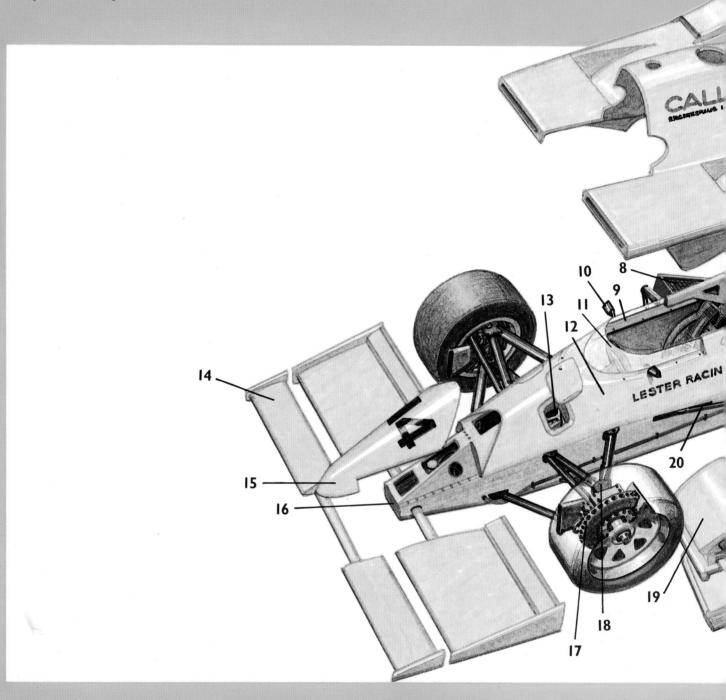

1	Low drag speedway rear wing	9	Reinforced anti-intrusion cockpit surround
2	High downforce road-circuit rear wing	10	Rearview mirror
3	Airscoop for turbocharger and gearbox oil cooler	11	Quick release steering wheel
4	Plenum chamber	12	Carbon fiber monocoque top, bonded to aluminum honeycomb lower tub
5	Boost pressure control valve		
6	Fuel vent. Tank capacity 40 U.S. gallons	13	Right-hand coil spring-damper unit
7	Refueling inlet blanking plate. Valve may be fitted to left or right side	14	Speedway front wing
		15	Carbon fiber nose molding
8	Engine water radiator	16	Strengthened nose box

17	Front ventilated disc brake and caliper	
18	Front suspension upper and lower wishbones and pull-rod	
19	Right-hand sidepod and radiator duct	
20	Gearshift linkage	
21	Engine oil cooler	
22	Mechanical fuel pump and filter	
23	Lucas capacitor discharge ignition system	
24	Cosworth DFX Turbo engine 2.65 liters, 161 cubic inches	

25	Turbo intake
26	Rear suspension lower wishbone
27	Rear ventilated disc brake and caliper
28	Rear suspension rocker arm
29	Turbocharger
30	March five-speed and reverse gearbox

The **Indianapolis 500** is the best-attended sporting event in all of the United States. Each Memorial Day weekend over 400,000 fans show up at the Indianapolis Speedway. Millions more watch this great championship on their home televisions. The Indy 500 is also one of the richest races in the world. It boasts the largest purse, or prize money, in automobile racing, with the 33 competitors sharing up to $4 million. The first driver to complete the 500 miles—200 laps

around the 2½-mile track—takes home more than $500,000. Even the last-place finisher receives over $75,000.

When the first Indy 500 was held in 1911, the winner, Ray Harroun, took over 6½ hours to complete the race, averaging just under 75 mph. Today's champions are about twice as fast, completing the Indy 500 in about 3½ hours, averaging 152 mph!